The Anointi

Maintaining a Fresh Anointing

for Everyday Living

Michael Haile

GGMI 2022

The Anointing Within

Maintaining a Fresh Anointing for Everyday Living

Michael Haile

GGMI 2022

GGMI is a Christian ministry founded by Michael Haile in 2018 to be a conduit for the glory of God to reach the masses. Michael teaches in churches, prisons, seminars and conferences, with emphasis on the power of the Holy Spirit.

Unless otherwise indicated, all Scripture quotations are taken from the New King James Version of the Bible.

Table of Contents

Dedication

I dedicate this book to my mother, who is an epitome of integrity. My mother has stood by me through thick and thin, and this is a little token of my appreciation for everything she has been and done for me throughout my life.

I want to thank Lemi my wife and children - Ruth, Liz, Sam, and Hannah - for their love and amazing patience over the years. They have been supportive of my many projects whether they succeeded or not, which meant so much to me, and with this project that is close to my heart, I thank them for their help - from proofreading my manuscripts to encouraging me in my many endeavours.

I thank my pastor, my close friends and family, for their support in the production of this book. I hope that they, along with my readers, will be blessed through its message.

Foreword

Are you tired of struggling and fighting vigorously or striving only to see little fruit? The Anointing Within is the key that unlocks the Christian way of life.

Many Christians are not aware of this amazing potential that is available to them to help meet various needs – from personal to those of nations.

Pastor Michael will take you deeper into knowing the Almighty Third Person of the Trinity, Who is our access to intimacy with the Lord, the gateway to divine power and our license to serve the Lord.

'The Anointing Within' opens the door to the wonderful freedom that the grace of God offers to every believer in Jesus Christ.

Pastor Zinaw Tessema

Senior Pastor and founder
Holiness unto the Lord International Church, UK

Preface

My people are destroyed for lack of knowledge.

(Hosea 4:6, NKJV)

I was compelled to write this book for two reasons. One was to help believers, especially young believers, understand the value of pursuing God privately, by taking responsibility for their spiritual walk to a desired end – more of God's power manifested in their daily lives.

The second reason is to bring some balance to the erroneous culture that has engulfed some churches, and the spiritual trend that so many believers seem to be following nowadays which has shifted the focus away from the Lord Jesus Christ. There has been an unhealthy emphasis on the ministry of prophets, apostles, men of God, pastors and so on. Some men have crept in unnoticed bringing with them unscriptural practises that bring no honour to our Saviour; on the contrary, with the profuse use of social media, the church by in large has faced embarrassment and ridicule. This has been Satan's strategy all along, to get people to admire a man or a woman in the place of God, to accept practises that grieve the Holy Spirit, and to depend on a so-called prophet for guidance.

It is never God's desire that His people lack any knowledge, especially concerning spiritual matters. He wants us to be adequately prepared to do His will in the earth. After all, this was why He set the ministry gifts in the church – to edify believers, not to enslave them.

As you read this book, it is my desire that you begin to develop a passion to walk with God personally by praying and reading His word. I encourage you to serve God in your local church, but the primary way you will experience God's anointing is when you put first things first – a private prayer life.

Yours in Christ

Michael Haile

Chapter One: What is the Anointing?

The anointing is the manifested power of God

The anointing is the power of God. It is a limited power that God sends to the Earth for a limited time to accomplish a specific purpose. Jesus Christ, the Son of the Living God, is the only One Who was anointed without measure. (John 3:34)That is why He was able to "lay His hand on every one of them and heal them." (Luke 4:40) Believers however are anointed with a measure. God gives us a measure of faith, a measure of grace and a measure of anointing. Not one of us has it all. This measure of anointing is given to us to perform an act, accomplish a purpose or destroy the works of the devil. Whatever avenue God chooses to use to manifest His anointing, it brings a profit, an edification, or a healing. *"But the manifestation of the Spirit is given to each one for the **profit** of all" (1 Corinthians 12:7 NKJV)* The anointing then is a supernatural manifestation of God's power in the life of a believer to bring about healing - whether spiritual or physical.

Notable Bible teachers agree that there are two categories of anointings: the anointing **within** and the anointing **upon**. The anointing that came on the 120 believers on the day of Pentecost was the power of God that they received when the Holy Spirit came **upon** them. It was a distinct supernatural manifestation of God that they experienced when the Holy Spirit came upon them. This was not a metaphor, but an actual endowment of the believers with a heavenly reality that they felt, resulting in their lives being changed dramatically.

The Bible uses certain words interchangeably to refer to the Anointing:

Unction or anointing (1 John 2:20)

The Holy Spirit (Romans 15:13)

Power (Ephesians 3:20)

Gift (2 Timothy 1:6)

The Anointing Upon

"But you shall receive **power** when the **Holy Spirit** has come **upon you**." (Acts 1:8, NKJV)

We can see this experience recurring in Acts, indicating that this endowment of power on believers through the anointing that comes upon us is not a one-time experience.

"And when they had prayed, the place where they were assembled together was shaken; and they were all **filled with the Holy Spirit**, and they spoke the word of God with boldness" (Acts 4:31-33 NKJV)

Notice what happened after they were filled with the Holy Spirit. They went out and spoke the word of God with boldness. They were empowered to do the work of an evangelist. The anointing that fell upon them was for the work of the ministry.

"And the **Spirit of the Lord** came mightily **upon him,**
and he tore the lion apart as one would have torn apart
a young goat, though he had nothing in his hand."

(Judges 14:6, NKJV)

The anointing that fell on Samson was what the Bible calls the gift of the working of miracles. It empowered Samson to do a supernatural act for a specified period. The anointing did not stay with him day and night. In the above verse, Samson was given a divine ability that enabled him to tear the lion without a weapon. You'll agree I'm sure that this was a mighty act.

The '**Anointing Upon**' is primarily for the purpose of ministry, usually public ministry. An individual believer receives an anointing from God, an endowment from Heaven, that enables him or her to perform a duty supernaturally. This is certainly the case with the fivefold ministry, namely the offices of the Apostle, Prophet, Evangelist, Pastor and Teacher. Each of these ministry gifts is a supernatural placement of an office by God Himself within His church. An individual cannot make himself a prophet, for instance; or you cannot call yourself to any of these offices. The anointing for the office of an evangelist, for example, enables the preacher to convey the message of the cross in such a way that it is understood by the listeners so that they receive faith to be saved. Furthermore, the office of an evangelist always is accompanied by healings, signs, and wonders. If a so-called evangelist does not have signs and wonders operating in their ministry, then really, they are not true evangelist (they may just be exhorters according to Romans 12:8)

A marvellous example of a true evangelist who had an anointing upon him was Philip.

*"Then Philip went down to the city of Samaria and **preached Christ** to them. And the multitudes with one accord heeded the things spoken by Philip, hearing and seeing the **miracles** which he did. For **unclean spirits**, crying with a loud voice, **came out of many** who were possessed; and **many** who were **paralyzed**, and **lame***

*were **healed**. And there was great joy in that city."* (Acts
8: 5-6, NKJV)

Philip was anointed with power to heal the sick, cast out devils and perform miracles. Notice the evil spirits came out while Philip was preaching Christ to the Samaritans. The anointing upon Philip began working among the people as that was his ministry gift. This was not an anointing within; it was only activated when Philip began to preach. In other words, this anointing upon him did not operate when, for instance, Philip was at home talking with his family. This is one of the major differences between the two types of anointings:

The anointing within is for personal benefit, while the anointing upon is for ministry.

The laity are anointed too

The anointing upon is not exclusive to the fivefold ministry gifts. Let's look at other example in the Word of God.

"Having then **gifts** differing according to the grace that is given to us, let us use them: if prophecy, let us prophesy in proportion to our faith; or ministry, let us use it in our ministering; he who teaches, in teaching; he who exhorts, in exhortation; he who gives, with liberality; he who leads, with diligence; he who shows mercy, with cheerfulness." (Romans 12: 6-8, NKJV)

Any believer can prophesy if they are anointed by God, but they must do so in accordance with their faith. It is interesting to see here that leadership within a local church is an anointing that God bestows upon an individual. That means Pastors are responsible to ensure only those with a leadership anointing are put in positions of authority to help lead the local church.

Once again, an anointing is a portion of God's power that comes upon an individual to help him or her perform a particular task supernaturally.

The Anointing Within

It seems believers are more familiar with the anointing upon, than they are with the anointing within. The truth is we all have this power within us already – if we are born again, but few seem to be benefitting from it. I believe the main reason is a lack of biblical knowledge about it. Let's go back to the title of this book – "**The anointing within**". There is an anointing within you right now, according to 1 John 2:20

You already have an anointing within you, the power of God residing in you right now. This is profound, and if it weren't clearly stated in Scripture, would have been presumptuous. But you do have the power of God, an anointing, in you right now. It is not possible to be anointed from above at will; even if you pray all week long, there's no guarantee that you will be anointed from above with an 'anointing upon'. But you can be certain you have an anointing in you. Well, what does this mean? It means there is a supernatural power in you that you can utilise daily. We are not talking about ministry here, rather experiencing the power of God to help you live spiritually strong every day.

You have God's power, His supernatural ability **right now**. You're not trying to manufacture anything. It is a settled and scriptural fact that the power of God is in you now if you are a new creation in Christ Jesus.

Say this out loud to yourself: "*I have the anointing of God within me*"

Chapter Two: God Anoints for a Purpose

The anointing enables us to perform a task supernaturally

Everything God does has a purpose behind it. Everything. The Holy Spirit, Who is the Power of the Godhead, came to the Earth to help the church. *The church is never without help.* But like everything else in the bible, this power also is accessed through faith. But before we study how this power is accessed, let's see what it does.

The anointing teaches

"I still have many things to say to you, but you cannot bear them now. However, when **He, the Spirit of truth**, has come, **He will guide you** into all **truth** ..." (John 16:13, NKJV)

The Holy Spirit is the Spirit of Truth. He is the One who enables believers to comprehend what Jesus Christ did on the cross, which the world considers foolishness. It is impossible for us to appreciate the substitutionary sacrifice of Jesus through His blood – without the spiritual understanding that the Holy Spirit brings. Even the Lord Jesus Himself was not able to convey all He wanted to His disciples so He said, "*I still have many things to say to you, but you cannot bear them now.*" Spiritual truths are discerned spiritually and require the work of the Holy Spirit.

Have you ever wondered how some people cannot seem to understand the truths of the Word of God no matter how hard you try to explain to them? You wonder how it is that they cannot grasp simple concepts such as faith, for instance. The answer is the anointing. It is impossible to understand the things of God mentally because God's truths must be revealed, and it is the Holy Spirit Who reveals. He does this by guiding us into "**all truth**".

I remember years ago experiencing this work of God's anointing in my personal life. I had just repented of a particular sin that had grieved the Lord and even though

I believed I was forgiven I had a hard time forgetting about it and was feeling quite low. I thought about the verse in Romans 8:28

"And we know that **all things work together for good** to those who love God, to those who are the called according to His purpose." (Romans 8:28. NKJV)

I asked the Lord if this included the sin that I had just repented of. I said to the Lord, "*Lord, You said in your Word that all things work together for good. Does 'all' include sin? I don't think it does, but Romans 8:28 says 'all'. And I think all means all, but please show me in Your Word if this is so.*" I prayed this prayer early one evening thinking the Lord would answer me right then, but nothing happened. The next morning, during my time of devotion, I suddenly heard the Holy Spirit say, "*read the book of beginnings*", referring to the Gospel of Matthew. While I turned to Matthew in my Bible, the Holy Spirit said, "*and do not skip any verses*". That was quite funny because I never liked the first chapter of Matthew because people are always begetting people, and I could not figure out why that was written. I had no interest in who begat who, so I would always skip the begetting part when reading Matthew. But this time, the Lord said, *"don't skip it"*.

Understand this. The Holy Spirit will always lead you in line with Scripture. He will never tell you anything that would contradict the Word of God. He will never tell you to divorce your wife. Some of the things people say that the Holy Spirit told them do not line up with God's truths in the Bible. If you ask the Holy Spirit to teach you, He will do so because He has already given you an anointing, and the anointing teaches you all things.

> "But you have an **anointing** from the Holy One,
>
> and you know all things." (1 John 2:20, NKJV)

We have received an unction, an anointing that teaches us all things. *You are never without help*.

Back to Matthew. I began to read, and the following verse jumped out at me:

"... and Jesse begot David the king. David the king begot Solomon by her who had been **the wife of Uriah**."

(Matthew 1:6)

I saw it! I went to the Old Testament to read this account of David's life, even though I'd read it before. I found out that David committed a horrible sin by taking someone else's wife, attempted to cover up his adultery and when he failed, he had her husband (Uriah) killed. The woman of course is Bathsheba, and we know that David later married her, and she gave birth to Solomon, whom the Bible calls the wisest and richest person who ever lived. That's what the Lord meant *all things work together for good* – if we love Him and are called according to His purpose.

I cannot emphasise enough what this experience did to me. The doubts and insecurities I had following my repentance just dissolved. I also had a greater appreciation for the anointing of the Holy Spirit which was already in me, and the Holy Spirit seemed so close to me than ever before. In my case, this revelation of God's Word enabled me to trust God with my life no matter what I go through, and that He can turn any negative event into something good – if I love Him.

I shared the above simple experience from my own life to make this point: *the anointing is for every believer* with its primary benefit being understanding of Scripture as it pertains to your personal life. Secondly, the anointing brings clarity to scriptures you already know, meaning the anointing will never bring a revelation that does not line up with the written Word of God. Thirdly, this anointing within you will not work unless you activate it. In my example, *the anointing was activated through prayer* – a simple request I made to God.

The anointing empowers

"Finally, my brethren, **be strong** in the Lord and **in the power** of His might." (Ephesians 6:10)

This is a familiar verse to most of us. It is one of the most vital portions of Scripture God wrote for us if we can utilise it. So, God says, "Be strong". Notice God is telling weak people to be strong. If we were already strong, He wouldn't be telling us to be strong. There is a clue in this verse that indicates *how* we are to be strong. "...*in the power of His might*" Whose might? His might. The Holy Spirit's might.

> "Now to Him who is able to do exceedingly abundantly above all that we ask or think, **according to the power that works in us** ..." (Ephesians 3:20)

This power or might is found in us. According to the power ... in us. You already have the power of God, or His might, in you. God put it in there, in your spirit. It is an established fact. You have the power of God residing in you. The anointing of God lives in you. It is this anointing that strengthens you. When God tells you to be strong, He is not telling you to be strong in your own strength. I like the Amplified version of this verse:

"In conclusion, **be strong in the Lord** [draw your strength from Him and be empowered through your union with Him] and in **the power of His** [boundless] **might**." (Ephesians 6:10, AMP)

The anointing empowers. This is a spiritual and supernatural strength you can experience daily. You do not have to go through down, depressed, and confused days. You don't have to be under the weather. You can experience God's supernatural strength every day of your life, and you do this through the anointing within you – if you work it!

Say this out loud, *"the anointing of God is in me, and I am strong in the Lord"*

The anointing reveals

Another characteristic of the anointing is that it reveals. Revelation is an important part of what God wants to do in your life. There are so many things you can never learn mentally. The things of God must be revealed.

"When Jesus came to the region of Caesarea Philippi, he asked his disciples, "Who do people say the Son of Man is?" They replied, "Some say John the Baptist; others say Elijah; and still others, Jeremiah or one of the prophets." "But what about you?" he asked. "Who do you say I am?" Simon Peter answered, "You are the Messiah, the Son of the living God." Jesus replied, "Blessed are you, Simon son of Jonah, for **this was not revealed to you by flesh and blood, but by my Father in heaven**." (Matthew 16:13-18, NKJV)

God reveals His mysteries to us through the Holy Spirit. These mysteries were hidden throughout the ages until the Lord Jesus came to the Earth to give His life as ransom. After His death, burial, and resurrection, He

18

ascended to Heaven and sent us His Holy Spirit, Who is our Helper. One of the ways He helps us is by revealing God's truth, because He is the Spirit of revelation.

> "...that the God of our Lord Jesus Christ, the Father of glory, may give to you **the spirit of wisdom and revelation** in the knowledge of Him ... (Ephesians 1:17, NKJV)

The Holy Spirit reveals. A revelation is a portion of God's knowledge that you receive supernaturally. Many people mentally assent to Scripture, but a revelation is something you receive directly from God through the Holy Spirit.

How do you know you're saved? How do you know you're a child of God? By revelation. A revelation of God makes a Scripture verse come alive in you; the verse is not just on the pages of the Bible; it now becomes a part of you. It is just as real to you as the person God spoke it to in the Bible. The anointing reveals.

Remember that the anointing is an antidote to the work of the devil. The devil hides, God's anointing reveals. The devil masquerades, God's anointing exposes. You can rely on the anointing of God in you.

This anointing extends to our personal lives too. Many years ago, I was at a prayer meeting in someone's house where we just fellowshipped and prayed. During prayer I began to experience unsettling thoughts that a family member was in trouble. It wasn't a revelation in my spirit, it was a tormenting thought in my mind – and I could not focus on what we were praying about. So, I interrupted the prayer politely and asked everyone if we could pray for my family member. We began to pray in the Spirit and a few minutes later the Holy Spirit revealed to me that all was well. It was the devil who brought those fearful thoughts to my mind and that there was nothing wrong with the individual. That brought so much peace to my mind.

Understand this. ***God is a God of peace***. He will never trouble your mind. If you are confused, then God has nothing to do with it. Confusion does not come from God. If things are hidden, it is not God hiding it from you. God is the God of revelation.

Pray this prayer: "Father, grant to me the Spirit of wisdom and revelation, in Jesus Name."

Chapter Three: Faith and Prayer

Faith and Prayer unleash the anointing in you

The anointing is activated through two avenues: faith and prayer. We release our f*aith* through ***prayer***, then God releases His ***anointing***.

"But without faith it is impossible to please Him." (Hebrews 11:6)

You cannot get away from faith, even when it comes to the subject of the anointing. Let's look at a couple of accounts in the Bible that will teach us how the anointing works.

Your faith causes the anointing to work for you

Let's look at the account of the woman with the issue of blood as recorded in Mark 5: 25-34, NKJV.

Now a certain woman had a flow of blood for twelve years and had suffered many things from many physicians. She had spent all that she had and was no better, but rather grew worse. When she heard about Jesus, she came behind Him in the crowd and touched His garment. **For she said**, "If only I may touch His clothes, I shall be made well."

This woman had a need, a physical ailment, that only the supernatural power of God can heal. She was not being overly spiritual when she sought out God's help. She'd already tried medical help, but to no avail. Notice verse 28: "For she said..."

The major way the anointing is accessed is through faith, your own faith. But then, everything else you want from God is accessed through faith. You must settle this in your mind once and for all. God is a faith God. You cannot contact Him with your physical senses. No amount of praying will move God if the prayer is not mixed with faith. Your begging, feeling sorry for yourself, blaming others, even fasting will not move God an inch – if there is no faith at the centre of it.

"**Immediately the fountain of her blood was dried up**, and she felt in her body that she was healed of the affliction. And Jesus, immediately knowing in Himself that **power had gone out of Him**, turned around in the crowd and said, "Who touched My clothes?"

There's that word again – *power*. Power went out of Jesus and flowed into the woman. *You must understand that Jesus has all the power you need*. This woman understood Jesus had enough power in Him to rid her of her ailment. That difficult walk she made from her house to where Jesus was, was a walk of faith. And you must walk by faith too, if you want the power of God flowing into you. There is no sure way to experience the power of God for yourself without showing God your faith. God wants to see faith in your life before He manifests His power. He wants to shower you with all the power you can handle, but He must first be pleased with your faith walk. Notice the power went out of Jesus "immediately". That's different to what most preachers do today, isn't it?! There's not a lot of immediate power manifested in most churches; oh, the preacher may shout and holler but only with promises about the future. But this woman did not want healing in the future, she needed it now. And Jesus had all the power she needed. She was healed immediately.

How was she healed? The scriptures plainly tell us how!

And He looked around to see her who had done this thing. But the woman, fearing and trembling, knowing what had happened to her, came, and fell down before Him and told Him the whole truth. And He said to her, "Daughter, **your faith has made you well**. Go in peace and be healed of your affliction."

Her faith is how she got healed. You might say it's the power of God that healed her. Well yes, but don't forget that the power of God was available all the time wherever Jesus went, but with so many people thronging Jesus, only this woman tapped into the power of God, and she did that through her faith.

Faith connects you to the anointing

Now they came to Jericho. As He went out of Jericho
with His disciples and a great multitude, blind
Bartimaeus, the son of Timaeus, sat by the road
begging. And when he heard that it was Jesus of
Nazareth, he began to cry out and say, "Jesus, Son of
David, have mercy on me!" Then many warned him to
be quiet; but he cried out all the more, "Son of David,
have mercy on me!" So, Jesus stood still and
commanded him to be called. Then they called the blind
man, saying to him, "Be of good cheer. Rise, He is calling
you." And throwing aside his garment, he rose and
came to Jesus. So, Jesus answered and said to
him, "What do you want Me to do for you?" The blind
man said to Him, "Rabboni, that I may receive my sight."
Then Jesus said to him, "Go your way; **your faith
has made you well**." And immediately he received his
sight and followed Jesus on the road." (Mark 10: 46-52,
NKJV)

Your faith connects you to the power of God, or *the anointing*. There is no other way to tap into the anointing of God, apart from faith. Bartimaeus had a condition that could only be resolved if the anointing of God to heal was released on his behalf. He cried out and cried out some more. No doubt he begged and moaned. But in the final analysis, it was his faith that released the supernatural power of God from Jesus to him. Notice what Jesus said was responsible for the blind man's healing. "… *your faith has made you well.*" You and I know it was the anointing on Jesus that healed the man, but Jesus said the man's faith is responsible for the healing that was manifested.

Jesus can heal anyone of anything at any time. But he requires faith. *The anointing is released only for someone with faith*. Active faith.

Say this out loud, "*I believe.*"

God wants to see your faith before He gives you His power

"Now it happened on a certain day, as He was teaching, that there were Pharisees and teachers of the law sitting by, who had come out of every town of Galilee, Judea, and Jerusalem. And **the power of the Lord was present to heal** them. Then behold, men brought on a bed a man who was paralyzed, whom they sought to bring in and lay before Him. And when they could not find how they might bring him in, because of the crowd, they went up on the housetop and let him down with his bed through the tiling into the midst before Jesus." (Luke 5: 17-19, NKJV)

And the power of the Lord was present to heal. The house was crowded but nobody got healed until the man who was paralyzed was let down through the roof. Although the power of God was available, it was not manifested because there was no faith among the crowd. Think about this: Jesus was in a crowded room, and nobody got healed except the paralyzed man.

"**When He saw their faith**, He said to him, "Man, your sins are forgiven you." And the scribes and the Pharisees began to reason, saying, "Who is this who speaks blasphemies? Who can forgive sins but God alone?" But when Jesus perceived their thoughts, He answered and said to them, "Why are you reasoning in your hearts? Which is easier, to say, 'Your sins are forgiven you,' or to say, 'Rise up and walk'? But that you may know that the Son of Man has power on earth to forgive sins"—He said to the man who was paralyzed, "I say to you, arise, take up your bed, and go to your house." **Immediately he rose up** before them, took up what he had been lying on, and departed to his own house, glorifying God." (Luke 5:20-25, NKJV)

Faith connects you to the anointing of God, whether to the anointing upon or the anointing within.

God has the anointing you need, but do you have the
faith to receive?

Say this out loud, "I have faith to receive".

Prayer releases the anointing of God

The second way the anointing is accessed is through
prayer. The right kind of prayer helps you tap into the
supernatural power of God released in you and through
you.

"The effective, fervent prayer of a righteous man avails
much." (James 5:16, NKJV)

You can access the anointing of God for yourself by
praying the right way. I like the Amplified version of the
above verse.

"The heartfelt and persistent prayer of a righteous
man (believer) can accomplish much [when put into
action and made effective by God—it is dynamic and
can have tremendous power." (James 5:16, AMP)

The Passion translation says it this way:

> *"...tremendous power is released through the*
> *passionate, heartfelt prayer of a godly believer."*
> *(James 5:16, Passion)*

I like that! ***Tremendous power is released through prayer***. You can determine to pray effectively so that the power you need is released. Notice the criteria: the prayer must be heartfelt and persistent. You can access any amount of supernatural power or anointing you need – if you pray correctly.

Chapter Four: The Value of Speaking in Tongues

Speaking in tongues is the first step to the supernatural

This is such a vast topic that it will need another book, but we will only look at the benefits of speaking in tongues in relation to the anointing of God within you.

"And they were all **filled with the Holy Spirit** and began to **speak with other tongues**, as the Spirit gave them utterance." (Acts 2:4, NKJV)

The above verse is talking about the baptism of the Holy Spirit with the evidence of speaking in other tongues, which is a distinct experience that follows the new birth. It is an experience that you can have as a born-again believer, and it is an immensely beneficial one. In His wisdom, God decided that this would be the number one way that His people would receive supernatural strength for everyday living.

"However, we speak wisdom among those who are mature, yet not the wisdom of this age, nor of the rulers of this age, who are coming to nothing. But we speak **the wisdom of God** in a mystery, the hidden wisdom which God ordained before the ages for our glory, which none of the rulers of this age knew; for had they known, they would not have crucified the Lord of glory." (1 Corinthians 2:6-16, NKJV)

God's wisdom is a mystery to the world and to the natural mind. God's wisdom, or His way of doing things, is so vastly different to that of human beings, that it appears as foolishness. It is impossible to grasp God's infinite wisdom intellectually, especially His wisdom displayed in the redemptive work that Jesus accomplished, therefore it takes the work of the Holy Spirit and humility on our part to comprehend it. Everything about God is a mystery until the Spirit of revelation enlightens our spirits and illuminates our minds.

An astounding work that the Holy Spirit does in bringing the revelation of Jesus Christ to our spirits and minds then is through His anointing released in us as we pray in the Spirit, or tongues.

"For he who speaks in a **tongue** does not speak to men but to God, for no one understands him; however, **in the spirit he speaks mysteries**." (1 Corinthians 14, NKJV)

When you speak in tongues, you are speaking out the mysteries of God. They are not mysteries to God; they are only a mystery to your natural mind. But as you continue to speak in other tongues, the Holy Spirit will bring you a revelation, an enlightenment so that you receive an insight into the wonderful inheritance you have in Christ.

This is a work of the anointing of God within you that God really wants you to allow to function. Speaking in tongues is a very important part of our Christian walk. Believers usually fall on either side of the ditch when it comes to speaking with tongues. One side of the ditch is filled with believers who may have spoken in tongues at one point in the past, but they no longer exercise it. As a result, spiritual things are not exciting to them, and they are dull to the leading of the Holy Spirit. They may quote Scripture verses, but they do not have a spiritual glow. And then there are believers who fall into the other side of the ditch by over-emphasising the importance of speaking in tongues. Years ago, there was a popular teaching called 'warring tongues', where people would be instructed to pray against the devil by screaming and hollering at him in tongues. This of course is an unscriptural practise, and you won't find it in the Bible.

God wants us to be in the middle of the road on every subject of the Bible, including the wonderful practise of speaking in tongues. We should enjoy it and gain the most out of it, but not at the expense of other biblical truths.

"And pray in the Spirit on all occasions with **all kinds of prayers** and requests..." (Ephesians 6:18, NIV)

There are varying types of prayer, hence why the above verse says to pray with 'all kinds of prayers', and not just one type. We are to incorporate all types of prayer into our personal devotions, and not just praying in tongues.

Speaking in tongues strengthens the anointing

Speaking in tongues helps your spirit in two ways. First, it strengthens your faith. Now, faith does not come by praying in tongues, faith comes by hearing the Word of God. (Romans 10:17) When you speak in tongues, the faith that you already have begins to be strengthened. You begin to develop spiritual stamina through faith.

"But you, beloved, **build**ing yourselves **up** on your most holy **faith, praying in the Holy Spirit**" (Jude 1:20, NKJV)

Praying in tongues builds you up or provides you with spiritual strength. The more you pray in other tongues, the stronger you will be spiritually. It is such a simple concept, but not many engage in this edifying experience. What will happen to you as you continue to be faithful in praying in tongues is that the Holy Spirit will move you in the things of God and you will begin to pray in the Spirit under an anointing. The Bible calls this 'speaking in different kinds of tongues'. (1 Corinthians 12:10, NKJV) This is where the Holy Spirit takes a hold of your spirit and prays out the will of God, either for you or someone else.

"Likewise, **the Spirit also helps** in our weaknesses. For **we do not know what we should pray for** as we ought, but the Spirit Himself makes intercession for us with groanings which cannot be uttered. Now He who searches the hearts knows what the mind of the Spirit is, because He makes intercession for the saints according to the will of God." (Romans 8:26-27, NKJV)

That anointing in you that you cultivated by praying in other tongues brings about a stronger unction so that the Holy Spirit prays through you the perfect will of God concerning a given situation.

I remember an event that happened some years back at an all-night prayer meeting. The leader asked me to join him to pray for some of the people who were present, and I began to pray for a few individuals one after the other. I walked up to a dear sister and began to speak in tongues while I laid my hand on her shoulder; I then began to sense an urgency in my spirit. It was a sense of grief in my spirit that indicated to me there was danger that the Holy Spirit wanted to avert.

Understand this: whatever the Holy Spirit tells you to do, you better do it. There are no trivial instructions from Him; everything He tells you to do is important, and at times it may be a matter of life and death. The number one way He tells you there is an issue to pray about is by sharing with you what He feels about that situation, usually a 'sense of danger' in your spirit. But you will never pick it up if you do not consistently pray in other tongues.

As I continued to pray for the woman, I hit a gusher as some old-time Pentecostals used to say. The horrible feeling in my spirit left and was instead replaced with joy and a sense of victory. The Holy Spirit never revealed to me what it was about, but I knew whatever it was, had now been dealt with, which is what I told her. I must have prayed for about ten or twelve minutes in the Spirit.

A few years later the lady told my wife and I what had happened. Her brother, who was not born-again, called her not long after the prayer meeting to tell her of how he literally escaped death. He was in a serious predicament facing certain death but was delivered suddenly. When she asked him when exactly God intervened, the day and time he told her was the exact time the Holy Spirit travailed through me. I did not know the prayer was for him. His own sister did not know the Holy Spirit was praying for him. Her brother himself did not know someone was praying for him. But God did, and God does. God always knows what to do in any situation. And He knows how to pray; we don't. So, what do we do when we don't know how to pray? We pray in tongues.

I can give you story after story of how speaking in tongues has benefited me personally, and I'm sure you have some stories too. The Holy Spirit is no respecter of persons. If you give time to pray in tongues, the anointing of God in you will flow up out of you to deliver someone. This anointing is so powerful there will be nothing the devil can do to stop it, but you must pray. If God shows you a dream where you saw someone in trouble, you better pray, and you better pray in the spirit, because if you don't, it will happen exactly as you saw it. Then you'll tell people that God showed you in a dream that so and so would lose their job, not knowing the reason He showed you was so you can pray in tongues long enough until the Holy Spirit made intercessions for the person to save them from losing their job. and He would have - had you prayed. God does not want you to be ignorant concerning spiritual things. Pray in tongues always.

Praying in tongues connects you to the anointing of God in you.

The more you pray in tongues, the greater His anointing will manifest in you and through you. When you don't know what to do, don't throw your hands in the air in discouragement. Instead, pray in tongues and listen to the leading of the Holy Spirit in your spirit. He will always guide you into all truth if you will give Him time.

You are anointed to pray. You have an anointing of God in you that enables you to pray according to the will of God. Yield to it today. Pray in the Spirit.

Say this out loud, *"I will pray in other tongues and build myself up spiritually"*.

Supernatural versus Spectacular

Sometimes we put a greater emphasis on a biblical topic than is merited. We tend to go to extremes instead of staying balanced. At times we may focus on the spectacular and miss the supernatural. People are more excited about hearing someone's testimony of an

41

angelic visitation or a vision but give little or no importance to praying in the Spirit or meditating on the Word. If you're not careful, you can focus on the spectacular so much that you miss the supernatural.

Speaking in tongues is a supernatural exercise. It is not spectacular or even sensational, nevertheless it is still supernatural. The utterances that the Holy Spirit gives you are supernatural. They are from another dimension, a world where God dwells. That makes speaking in tongues one of the most supernatural practises you can engage in, and you can do it daily.

"I thank my **God I speak with tongues** more than you all." (1 Corinthians 14:18, NKJV)

The apostle Paul, I'm sure you agree, was a phenomenal believer and minister of the Lord Jesus Christ who operated in signs and wonders consistently. He had an amazing revelation of the Gospel of God and the redemptive work of Jesus Christ. A practise that Paul engaged in day and night appears to be speaking in tongues. He said that he spoke in tongues more than all the believers in the church at Corinth. That is quite a statement because all the Corinthians seemed to have done was speak in tongues. The difference is that they did it in church and Paul did it privately. Always remember that the primary purpose of tongues (which some call their prayer language) is during your private devotion, usually by yourself, to fellowship with God your Father.

Chapter Five: Kings and Priests unto God

Every New Testament believer has received an anointing to be a king and a priest

"To Him who loved us and washed us from our sins in His own blood and has **made us kings and priests** to His God and Father, to Him be glory and dominion forever and ever. Amen" (Revelation 1:5-6, NKJV)

Praise and worship

"...so that the **priests** could not continue **ministering** because of the cloud; for the **glory** of the LORD filled the house of God." (2 Chronicles 5:14NKJV)

A priest ministers to the Lord. The above verse refers to Old Testament priests, but a priest's duty under the New Covenant hasn't changed when it comes to ministering to the Lord. Let's look at Acts 13:1

"Now in the church that was at Antioch there were certain prophets and teachers: Barnabas, Simeon who was called Niger, Lucius of Cyrene, Manaen who had been brought up with Herod the tetrarch, and Saul. **As they ministered to the Lord** and fasted, the Holy Spirit said, "Now separate to Me Barnabas and Saul for the work to which I have called them." Then, having fasted and prayed, and laid hands on them, they sent them away." (Acts 13: 1-3, NKJV)

"As they ministered to the Lord ..."

And how do you minister to the Lord? Through worship and prayer. God has given you an ability, a priestly anointing, to minister to Him. This is a heavenly anointing that you already have as a New Testament believer and a priest, that empowers you to offer acceptable sacrifices of worship.

"We have an altar from which those who serve the tabernacle have no right to eat. For the bodies of those animals, whose blood is brought into the sanctuary by the high priest for sin, are burned outside the camp. Therefore, Jesus also, that He might sanctify the

people with His own blood, suffered outside the
gate. Therefore, let us go forth to Him, outside the
camp, bearing His reproach. For here we have no
continuing city, but we seek the one to
come. Therefore, by Him let us continually offer the
**sacrifice of praise to God, that is, the fruit
of our lips, giving thanks to His name**." (Hebrews 13:10-
15, NKJV)

A priest offers the sacrifice of praise to God. You are
anointed to minister to the Lord by offering a sacrifice
of praise or worship.

In His presence there is fullness of joy

I have had some marvellous experiences in the Lord
over the years and most of them came about during
times of ministering to the Lord in praise and worship.
As I continued to worship Him for Who He is and What
He has done for me, His presence would come in and
just bless me. At times it would feel like rain droplets
that fell on top of me and permeate my being, and at

other times He would just fill my spirit with joy. There have been numerous occasions when His oil would visibly manifest on my fingertips and I would also feel oil being poured on my forehead. Many times, He would give me words of encouragement or a prophecy during these times of ministering to the Lord. I very much appreciate these special moments with the Lord and some experiences are quite sacred. It is scriptural to expect the Lord to speak to you as you minister to Him.

"As they ministered to the Lord and fasted, the Holy Spirit said"

This anointing is designed to bring the presence of God to you until your entire being is saturated with His manifested presence that it changes your entire outlook on life.

"In Your presence is **fullness of joy**;
At Your right hand are pleasures forevermore." (Psalm 16:11, NKJV)

You can set aside time to minister to the Lord in praise and worship, and if you will be faithful to do that, it won't be long before you begin to experience the presence of God in a fresh way. The priestly anointing that God has already put in your spirit is ready to help you minister to the Lord. Worship God and see the presence and power of God invade your life.

The priestly anointing to pray and intercede

Prayer is our second duty (and privilege) as New Testament priests. God has given us the ability to pray.

Remember the anointing enables you to perform a task

The type of prayer we are referring to here is 'intercession', which is praying on behalf of someone else. Here is what God says about it in 1 Timothy 2:1-4

"Therefore, **I exhort first of all** that supplications, **prayers, intercessions**, and giving of thanks be made for all men, for kings and all who are in authority, that we may lead a quiet and peaceable life in all godliness and reverence. For this is good and acceptable in the sight of God our Saviour, who desires all men to be saved and to come to the knowledge of the truth."

(NKJV)

We are commanded to intercede for all people, especially for those in authority over us; that means Presidents, Prime Ministers, Members of Parliament, Councillors, Judges, School Principals, Police Commissioners and so on. God tells us the reason:

"... that we may lead a quiet and peaceable life in all godliness and reference"

You look around some cities in the world and you'd wonder if there's anyone praying for the leaders of those cities because there's so much rampant crime, corruption, and violence. Nothing will change in the world until Christians intercede for their leaders in authority. Nothing. Pray for people. Pray for leaders. It is a command of God and you have been anointed to do it. Read the account of Abraham standing in the gap for a couple of cities in Genesis 18:16-33 and you will be amazed at the amount of spiritual authority he exercised before God by humbly pleading that God spare the cities from destruction. God seemed to agree with Abraham's intercession until he asked for mercy if ten righteous men were found in the cities. Then Abraham stopped praying. I'm not sure why he stopped at ten, but you can readily see how powerful intercession can be in averting even God's judgement on a city.

The priestly anointing to be a witness

"But you be watchful in all things, endure afflictions, **do the work of an evangelist**, fulfil your ministry." (2 Timothy 4:5, NKJV)

In addition to ministering to the Lord, priests also instruct sinners in the ways of righteousness; in other words, believers witness to those who are not born-again by telling them of the wonderful love of God and how they can be saved through faith in Jesus Christ.

Let's now consider what God said about Levi the priest in the book of Malachi:

> "The law of truth was in his mouth,
> And injustice was not found on his lips.
> He walked with Me in peace and equity,
> **And turned many away from iniquity**." (Malachi 2:6, NKJV)

You have been anointed to turn many away from iniquity. James 5:20 says, *"he who turns a sinner from the error of his way will save a soul from death and cover a multitude of sins."* (NKJV)

You may not be called to be an Evangelist, but you are encouraged by God to "do the work of an evangelist". You can do this by praying for and witnessing to the people in your sphere of influence. You have an anointing in you that will enable you to tell others about Jesus.

Shortly after I got saved, I joined a group of fervent Christians in the church I attended. We would go out to the streets to evangelise, which I found quite daunting as I was not bold to tell strangers about Jesus, nor had I had any background in public speaking. I was quite timid. I then found out that all I had to do was be brave enough to begin a conversation and it seemed this invisible cloud would come and envelope me and every trace of fear would simply vanish. That was the anointing, although I did not realise it at the time.

The Kingly anointing

The Bible says Jesus has made us kings unto God. We are royalty. We are kings and the Lord is the King of Kings.

"To Him who loved us and washed us from our sins in His own blood and has made us **kings** and **priests** to His God and Father, to Him be glory and dominion forever and ever. Amen" (Revelation 1:5-6, NKJV)

Kings rule. Kings reign. Kings have subjects. Kings give orders. And kings have a domain.

You have a domain. Your domain is the sphere of influence that God gave you. If you have a family, then you have a kingly anointing to govern members of your family. Your words have impact on each member of your family. Now, your family members are not your subjects. Some years ago, there was a very popular subject in some circles with regards submission. Husbands would yell at their wives and make them a nervous wreck in the guise of 'wives should submit to their husbands.' This erroneous teaching has resulted in divorces, premature deaths, untold misery, and a reproach among unbelievers.

Husbands are to govern their own homes by exercising love and self-control. Their subjects are not members of their family. Their subjects are devils and demons. The kingly anointing on the husband and wife brings divine protection on the family unit. This anointing drives away dark forces who attack families night and day.

Chapter Six: A Fresh Anointing

Just as a car needs a change of oil, we also need a refill of oil – a fresh anointing

"I am anointed with **fresh oil**." (Psalm 92:10, ASV)

Have you ever spoken to someone who used to be so on fire for God at one point in their life, but now they seem dry and uninterested in the things of God?! Sure, they may still go to church and even serve but they're not as fervent as they used to be. The sparkle in their eyes is gone and there's no spring about their step. You wonder what happened to them! What happened is that they lost their fresh anointing, and they need a refill.

God anoints us with fresh oil. If we do not get refreshed with His oil periodically, then we end up with stale oil.

Your car, if you have one, is supposed to get an MOT test or annual servicing to make it road worthy. The dashboard behind your steering wheel will show you what level the engine oil is at and if low, you will need to refill. Better yet, when servicing it, the old and stale oil is removed and replaced with new and fresh oil. The car runs so much better with fresh oil.

Similarly, we live so much better when we maintain a fresh oil in our spirits. The anointing brings a supernatural joy that enables us to weather any storm. Remember that being anointed within is not a one-time experience. It is a continual refilling of God's power that makes us walk strong in a dark world filled with adversity, and to do so with joy.

No one wants to listen to a sad Christian

The world is looking for joy, but in the wrong places. People go to bars, pay to see a stand-up comedian, or watch Tik Tok for hours on end – all searching for happiness. They do not know that there is joy available for free and that they don't need to seek happiness. Christians are responsible to walk full of the Holy Spirit so that unbelievers see their joy and be attracted to the message of Jesus. If your life does not match what you preach, then no one is going to listen to you.

"At that time Jesus, **full of joy through the Holy Spirit**, said, "I praise you, Father, Lord of heaven and earth, because you have hidden these things from the wise and learned, and revealed them to little children. Yes, Father, for this is what you were pleased to do." (Luke 10:21, NIV)

Jesus was the most joyful individual on the planet. People followed Him daily because He had an anointing of the Holy Spirit. You cannot be anointed and sad at the same time. This is worth repeating.

You cannot be anointed and sad at the same time

Notice the verse above: "... full of joy ..."

You can be full of joy, half full, a quarter full, or empty. How full of joy you are depends on your fellowship with the Holy Spirit. The Holy Spirit is the Spirit of joy. The more you spend time with the Lord by worshipping Him, praying in tongues, and meditating on His word – the more of God's fresh oil comes upon you. Stay in God's presence until His fresh anointing pours on you.

Say this out loud: "Father, anoint me with fresh oil today, in Jesus Name."

Chapter Seven: Practical steps to flow in your Anointing

The spiritual precedes the natural

"...be filled with the Spirit." (Ephesians 5:18, NIV)

God commands us to be filled with the Spirit. This is an experience that each of us can have each day by praying, worshipping God, reading His Word, and **speaking to ourselves**. Being full of the Holy Spirit results in a life filled with peace, joy, and supernatural strength. But what is the purpose?

"Wherefore be ye not unwise but understanding what the will of the Lord is. And be not drunk with wine, wherein is excess; but **be filled with the Spirit**; **Speaking to yourselves** in psalms and hymns and spiritual songs, singing and making melody in your heart to the Lord; Giving thanks always for all things unto God and the Father in the name of our Lord Jesus Christ; Submitting yourselves one to another in the fear of God"

(Ephesians 5: 17-21, KJV)

God wants us to be filled with the Spirit. You are always filled with something. There are no grey areas. God advises, "be filled with the Spirit". We do this by "*speaking to yourselves ...*"

Speaking is one way we activate the anointing in our lives. You cannot be quiet and expect God's help. You must walk your floor speaking the things of God and establishing the Word of God over your situation. You must tell God you want His power and that you are desperate for His anointing to be manifested in you. If you don't speak, you won't get much from Heaven. Speak the things of God.

If I ever feel down or despondent, I just start speaking words from the Bible and not long after I will begin to sense the anointing of God bubble up out of me. Many times, I would end up laughing out of my spirit. In the natural there may be nothing to laugh about; on the contrary, I may be facing several challenges all at once; but after a few minutes of confessing God's word and speaking in other tongues, the anointing in me begins to work and the joy of the Lord fills my being. Soon, I would be thanking God out loud and the burden that'd been weighing on me just rolls off me like water off a duck's back.

There are several ways that we can pursue to function in the anointing that God has for us, but we must put spiritual matters first, that's why being filled with the Spirit is crucial before you pursue the giftings God has given you.

Remember that an anointing is also called a 'gift'. This is the ability that God has placed in you that helps you function whatever your field of work or profession is.

Bold in church, fearful in the world

It seems to me that most church members shout and scream when praying inside a church building, 'believing' and claiming all kinds of breakthroughs and they get 'blessed' each week, then they do the same thing the next week, and the next. A whole year passes by with no real change, and the next new year is welcomed with much anticipation and sincere hope, and of course even more excitement, but oftentimes no action.

Now I'm not against shouting! You can shout until your voice is hoarse and then you can hop on a horse and ride to the mountains. But unless you do something when you come out of the church, nothing is changing.

Praying, or I should say the right kind of praying, brings the power of God. But then what are you going to do with the power of God? God gives you His power so that you do something with it in the workplace, the marketplace and anywhere else you happen to be during the week!

You need the anointing to be successful

The Word of God tells us to be filled with the Spirit and then follows it up with why He wants us to be full of the Holy Spirit.

"Don't just do what you have to do to get by, but **work heartily**, as Christ's servants doing what God wants you to do. And **work with a smile on your face**, always keeping in mind that no matter who happens to be giving the orders, you're really serving God." (Ephesians 6: 6, MSG)

It takes the power of God to be able to do what the above verse says. How many of us who go to church and pray practise this verse? Well, if you're not acting on this verse habitually, then you will not be a candidate for promotion. You'll just keep praying every week, rebuking this devil and that spirit, and God will just let you do your own thing. The Lord told us to be filled with His Spirit so that we would be able to do this verse and qualify for a breakthrough in our career, business, and personal development.

Remember, **the spiritual precedes the natural**.

There are a few more things we can do to help us step into the gifting or anointing that God has placed in us.

1. Networking

> "As iron sharpens iron,
>
> so **a friend sharpens a friend**" (Proverbs 27:17, NLT)

Spending time with those who share our values brings an edification to our personal development. We feel free to be who we are when we are accepted and valued. It is easier to relate to someone who has similar aspirations as you do since it is more than likely that you both face similar challenges which brings you some comfort in knowing you are not the only one facing struggles. Even more helpful is finding someone who's faced similar setbacks as you currently do but has overcome those difficulties; their life can be a signpost for you, to give you some sense of direction, as well as motivating you to press on and not give up.

This is certainly true when it comes to pursuing a career, starting a business, or gaining a professional qualification. It seems accomplishing a venture is an immense challenge to many believers. I sincerely believe spending time with people who have already obtained what you're pursuing is necessary to give you that extra push for a breakthrough.

Some experiences may be bittersweet

Some years ago, two good friends of mine approached me to start a joint venture, an international start-up that imports a commodity for distribution. It was an attractive prospect although I had minimal business acumen; I relied on their trade expertise so I could focus on research, admin, promotions, negotiations, and digital marketing. We had several formal and informal meetings, brainstorming breakfasts, discussions with a prominent supplier and to top it all — we prayed for about an hour at my house. I was expecting to receive several thousand pounds from a banking institution in insurance refunds for a financial product I had bought many years prior, and I promised my business partners that I would contribute this as a working capital towards the start-up. I then worked on the project for three months non-stop until they came to my house one day to say that they no longer wanted to partner with me. Their reason was that God showed them not to continue in the business with me. Now, when someone says God told them something, then there's no room for discussion. You can't have a reasonable conversation and you will have to leave the matter alone. It would have been better and honest if they simply told me they were not happy to split the profits three-ways.

Pain is inevitable, but misery is not

It was one of the most disheartening experiences of my life. They were of course not being forthright, but they sugar-coated their real reason and came up with a superficial argument to make it look spiritual and acceptable. It is entirely possible God wanted us to go our separate ways, however He does not bring division between brothers. Furthermore, they broke a covenant that we made before God and despised the fellowship we enjoyed in the presence of the Lord. Looking back though, they were a Godsend and I'm glad they started me off; I am certain the Lord sent them my way to awaken His purposes in me, however painful the experience was.

Leave the past behind

It took a few weeks to get my head clear enough to think about going forward. With encouragement from my family, I pursued the line of business that I started with my former partners, this time on my own. I found myself spending time with like-minded individuals who have been in the business for decades, which was an invaluable source of inspiration and direction for me. I was able to be quite proficient in the field in the space of two years or so. What seemed like the end of the world at the time proved to be the very avenue that propelled me into where I am today. If it weren't for my former partners, I would not have had numerous opportunities, contracts, trade deals and a large network of clients. Today, I thank God for them, and I thank Him even more that they gave me the push into the world of business.

The experience developed my ability to choose who to partner with, and who to avoid. This is not always easy since people can be phoney. But I have learnt to look for signs, ask questions, evaluate my relationships and most of all, have a set of values – one being, have everything in print and signed on the dotted line.

There are people who will support you; find them

I was amazed to find people that really cared, and many were outside of my familiar circles! Over a period of three years or so, I met entrepreneurs, multimillionaires, government officials, high profile stakeholders and business professionals; the amount of professional help, advice, and mentorship I received has been amazing.

We must find our support system, which may take some time, but it will be worth the wait once you locate the people you need. Not everyone is your friend, and you really don't need friends in business; you only need people you can trust. Find them, they will help you develop.

2. Just Do It

We all know Nike's slogan: "Just Do It"

Sometimes you must step out and just do it. You've done your research, you've made your analysis, you've read books, you've prayed about it …

You've done everything except doing it. Too much analysis can hinder you if it's not followed by an action of some sort. Stepping out does not necessarily mean throwing caution to the wind; you can have a phased approach to your project so that you minimise risks while making manageable progress.

So, just do it

Allow me to use another example to stress the importance of being practical. One of the gifts that I believe God gave me is helping people develop their leadership skills both in the church and the marketplace. Presently I may not be able to do this on a large scale, but I can conduct mini seminars and hope that they grow over time.

So, I just went for it. I asked a good minister friend of mine to announce to his church members if the businesspeople among his congregation would like to come to a leadership seminar. It was a simple announcement. I had no way of knowing how many people would turn up. I then prepared a set of notes and paid a designer to publish quality brochures that had a business feel to them. Next was the venue. Hotels are quite expensive, plus I was not charging anything for my services, so booking a hall was not feasible. So, I employed persuasive skills that I thought I had little of. Senior personnel at a prestigious hotel agreed for me to use one of their VIP lounges for free. More people than I anticipated came to the seminar, which was amazing. The attendees said they enjoyed the session; what they didn't know was that it was my first ever session. A major victory. Fear was overcome. All because I just did it.

Sometimes you just have to step out in faith, and the gift in you will begin to show up and develop. You will be surprised.

3. Self-Control (and cautious fasting)

Now this is an exercise you will need to practise with caution, and only if you are up to it and if there are no medical reasons why you should not fast. Fasting is a biblical practise that the Word of God encourages us to undertake periodically. This practise has many benefits but to name them all is beyond the scope of this book, so I will only discuss one of them.

Fasting makes you sensitive to the things of God

Fasting does not change God. God loves you before you fast, while you're fasting and after you fast. But fasting changes you. As you abstain from what your body needs for nourishment and focus on prayer and the Word of God, even for one day, you will become more in tune with the plans and purposes of God for your life. This includes the anointing that God has placed within you.

I find that one of the questions many people, especially young people, ask is: "What does God want me to do with my life". This is especially so when it comes to career choices. Fasting enables you to put your focus on God by putting away doubts and fears, so you can hear

God clearly. It is not a cure-all method, but it helps immensely if properly used.

Fasting periodically will increase the intensity of the anointing in you.

God does not want you to be flaky; do everything in moderation and His blessing will fall on you. Fasting is one of those personal and sacred acts that we do, usually secretly so that God rewards us publicly.

"But you, when you fast, anoint your head and wash your face, so that you do not appear to men to be fasting, but to your Father who *is* in the secret *place;* and your Father who sees in secret will reward you openly." (Matthew 6: 17-18, NKJV)

As you begin to add fasting to your spiritual walk, you will be amazed at the progress you will make with God, as well as in your personal life.

Say this out loud: *"Greater is He Who is in me than he who is the world. I can do all things through Christ Who strengths me. I am strong in the Lord and in the power of His might. The Holy Spirit lives in me and He is giving me all the strength I need. I am never without help. The Helper lives in me."* Praise God.

Chapter Eight: Hindrances

There are negative forces that block your anointing if you allow them

There are several obstacles that hinder the anointing from functioning in your life. I will however focus on three elements that I believe are major hindrances, and these are *fear, ignorance, and unbelief*.

Fear quenches the anointing

It is said that the phrase "Fear not" is mentioned in the Bible 365 times, one for each day; I'm not sure whether that's the case but the phrase certainly appears repeatedly. Many times, God opens a conversation with an individual with a "Fear not". Fear is an enemy. To tell the truth about it, fear is an entity, a being, a spirit.

*"For God has not given us a **spirit of fear**…" (2 Timothy 1:7, NKJV)*

God calls fear a spirit. If you are battling with fear, it did not come from God. Fear manifests itself in varying forms. Intimidation is one. Confusion is another. Fear aims to quench the anointing in you from coming forth. You will never be happy if you are not able to release the gift that God has placed in your spirit. The anointing within you must be allowed to flow out of you to bless others, but fear will keep it from being released. That's why you must guard your mind against the spirit of fear.

I remember years ago shortly after I got saved, I sometimes would battle against fear during times of prayer. It took me awhile to identify what it really was, and my victory came when the Holy Spirit highlighted a Scripture verse to me about the situation. Many years have come and gone, and that spirit of fear has never bothered me again.

Fear cripples. It paralyses you if you give place to it. It seems the number one way it operates is through a person of authority over your life. It is expressed either through direct and confrontational words or through indirect manipulation. Either way it is a strategy of the devil to keep you bound so that the anointing in you remains dormant.

Several years ago, I was getting ready to teach at a local church and throughout my journey to the venue I had such an unsettling and fearful feelings all over. The result was that I was not looking forward to ministering at all. I called a friend who was a prayer warrior and the Lord encouraged me through a prophetic word and the fear dispelled. My point is that fear is a spirit designed to attack the plans and purposes of God in you and you will have to resist it every day of your life. If you tolerate fear in your personal life, then the anointing within you will not be activated.

"Now to Him who is able to do exceedingly abundantly above all that we ask or think, **according to the power that works in us**." (Ephesians 3:20, NKJV)

You do have the power of God In you, according to Scripture, but is that power at work?! Whether God moves on our behalf depends not on the availability of His power in us, but whether that power is working. Is the anointing in you flowing or is it standing still?! Resist fear, and the power of God in you will work; it will empower you spiritually. You will not have beat down days, or blue Mondays. The power of God will strengthen you if you 'fear not'.

So, how do you 'fear not'?

"Therefore, I remind you to **stir up the gift of God** which is in you through the laying on of my hands. [7] For God has not given us a spirit of fear, but of power and of love and of a sound mind." (2 Timothy 1:6-7, NKJV)

God has not given to us the spirit of fear. What has He given us then? The Spirit of power! That's the anointing and it's in you. *But you must stir it up*. You have something to do with it. You cannot remain complacent. God says to stir up the anointing in you. That will take care of any fear you encounter.

Say this out loud, "*I refuse to fear.*"

Ignorance disconnects you from the anointing

"Now concerning spiritual gifts, brethren, **I do not want you to be ignorant**:" (1 Corinthians 12:1, NKJV)

God does not want you to be ignorant about anything, but especially concerning spiritual gifts. The word 'gifts' in the original is italicized, meaning it was added by the translators to help expound the verse. Therefore, the verse really is referring to spiritual things and not just spiritual gifts. God does not want us to be ignorant about spiritual things. In other words, God wants us to understand Him and His way of doing things.

Shortly after I started work fulltime, I wanted a change in careers, so I began to temp. My agency found me an accounting role at a junior level at a BBC charity and I worked there for three months. The organisation advertised the role on a permanent basis and of course I applied and was shortlisted. Several days before my line manager made the decision, the Lord awakened me one night (in a spectacular way, actually) because He wanted me to pray. I was quite immature in spiritual things in those days, and I could not make a connection in prayer with Him, so ignored His prompting. I was not selected and had to leave the company. The Finance Director spoke to me privately to say he'd expected me to get the job and had no idea why I was not selected. Obviously, the devil inspired the line manager not to approve my application, but I was too dumb to understand the Lord's direction, so the devil won in that instance.

Now let me share with you another incident which will show you what happens when we yield to the anointing of God in us. I was awakened one night and had a strong urge in my spirit to pray. No one wants to stay up at 1am in the morning but I knew better than to go back to sleep without praying, so I began to pray in other tongues because I had no idea why the Lord wanted me to pray. I must have prayed for 35 minutes before I hit a gusher; the urgency in my spirit lifted and I was filled with joy and began to laugh out of my spirit. I knew whatever the Lord wanted was done and I went back to sleep. A few days later the Lord delivered me from certain injury, or even possible death, when a gun shot was fired near our gate. I had planned to leave my house to go for a job interview, but the Lord brought an unusually heavy sleep on me, and I missed my appointment. The gunshot happened at our gate at the same time as when I'd originally planned to walk through it. I am totally satisfied that the Holy Spirit prayed out my deliverance several days beforehand.

"My people are destroyed for **lack of knowledge.**"
(Hosea 4:6, NKJV)

Lack of knowledge, or ignorance, will destroy you. Learn about God and His way of doing things. Learn to yield to the anointing of the Holy Spirit in you by praying in tongues daily. You will not regret it.

Say this out loud: "*I will yield to the Holy Spirit.*"

Unbelief nullifies the anointing

"Then He went out from there and came to His own country, and His disciples followed Him. And when the Sabbath had come, He began to teach in the synagogue. And many hearing Him were astonished, saying, "Where did this Man get these things? And what wisdom is this which is given to Him, that such mighty works are performed by His hands! Is this not the carpenter, the Son of Mary, and brother of James, Joses, Judas, and Simon? And are not His sisters here with us?" **So, they were offended at Him**. But Jesus said to them, "A prophet is not without honour except in his own country, among his own relatives, and in his own house." Now **He could do no mighty work** there, except that He laid His hands on a few sick people and healed them. [6] And **He marvelled because of their unbelief**."

We saw earlier that Jesus was anointed with the Holy Spirit and Power to heal the sick. (Acts 10:38) There were times when He healed everyone who touched him. In this case though, it says He could not do any mighty works except to lay His hands on a few sick people. The Word of God gives us the reason: 'because of their unbelief'!

Unbelief nullifies the anointing of God. Unbelief repels the power of God. Faith attracts the anointing; unbelief repels it. The sure way to get rid of unbelief is meditating on the Word of God and praying in the Spirit. I suppose we will always fight against unbelief to some extent, but God expects us to grow in faith and minimise the effects of unbelief so that we experience a greater measure of His anointing every day.

Chapter Nine: Quench not the Spirit

You will never be able to help God, but you can hinder Him by quenching His Spirit

"**Do not quench the Spirit**. **Do not despise** prophecies. Test all things; hold fast what is good. Abstain from every form of evil." (1 Thessalonians 5:19-22, NKJV)

As powerful as the Holy Spirit is, His works and anointings can be quenched if we're not careful. The Bible warns us, "Do not quench the Spirit". A synonym of 'quench' is: extinguish. You can extinguish the anointing of God in you. How? The next verse tells you how.

".. Do not despise …"

When your anointing is despised, it will be extinguished. This usually occurs when someone in authority, whether a parent or a church leader, despises what is in you. How much worse if you yourself despise the gift in you. Remember, spiritual things are real. A person can despise blatantly, or they can despise in their heart. They may smile and offer you a compliment, but since they despise you or your anointing, your gifting will be quenched if they have authority over you and you submit to them.

It seems some of us find it difficult to encourage fellow believers; some even suppose they have the gift of suspicion or the anointing to criticise. But fault-finding is never a godly attribute, neither is putting people down. How a person sees themselves directly impacts whether the gifting in them flows, therefore you should take extra care when speaking to those younger in the Lord than you. Build people up, do not tear them down. I've lost count of how many times I've heard people complain following a conversation they had with a church leader. They would feel discouraged or confused about a certain matter, which then stifles the gifting that God put in them. At times, they weren't even sure if their leader approved of their ministry, which can be quite depressing. You must encourage others if you desire to see them grow in what God has called them to do.

I remember a church service I attended many years ago. There was a guest speaker for that Sunday, but the pastor took up so much time with preliminaries, perhaps on purpose, that there really wasn't that much time left for the speaker. Even when the pastor called the speaker up to the stage, parents had to leave the service to go pick up their children from Sunday School. The speaker then stood behind the pulpit with head bowed and eyes closed, prayed privately for a few minutes, and just walked out of the church. Why? The anointing in her was despised. My friend, to make light of someone's anointing will put you on a collision course with God Himself. You will suffer needlessly, and God will hold you responsible for standing in His way.

Consider the following account in Matthew 3:13-17 and compare what was said by whom and you will see how important it is to discern the anointing in others.

"Then Jesus came from Galilee to John at the Jordan to be baptized by him. And **John tried to prevent Him**, saying, "I need to be baptized by You, and are You coming to me?" But Jesus answered and said to him, "**Permit it to be** so now, for thus it is fitting for us to fulfil all righteousness." Then he allowed Him. When He had been baptized, Jesus came up immediately from the water; and behold, the heavens were opened to Him, and [b]He saw the Spirit of God descending like a dove and alighting upon Him. And suddenly a voice came from heaven, saying, "This is My beloved Son, **in whom I am well pleased**."

Can you believe that John stood in the way of Jesus? He thought he was being humble when he hindered Jesus, just like some church leaders think they're being spiritual when they stop some members from prophesying – they do not know they are quenching the Holy Spirit. And John was working against the anointing without realising it. Jesus had to ask him to "permit it to be so now". John had the authority to say yes or to say no. And Jesus had to submit to John's authority. Jesus discerned the anointing on John and submitted to it.

Now look at what God the Father said about Jesus. He said, *"This is My beloved Son, **in whom I am well pleased**."* Can you picture what this affirmation would do to Jesus' confidence? And God did this publicly!

Encourage those under you in ministry and do so publicly. Rebuke privately but encourage publicly. You will see the anointing in them flourishing and you yourself will benefit from it.

Be faithful in little and God will reward you

Since we are primarily talking about the anointing in you and how it relates to your personal life, God expects you to honour His anointing in you even if you see little manifestations of it. Your tongues may be few syllables now, but do not despise them because they will increase if you are faithful. You may not have interpreted you tongues yet, but you will if you persist and do not give up.

Chapter Ten: Divine Order

God's divine order attracts the Anointing

"Behold, how good and how pleasant it is

For brethren to **dwell together in unity**!

It is like the precious **oil upon the head**,

Running down on the beard,

The beard of Aaron,

Running down on the edge of his garments.

It is like the dew of Hermon,

Descending upon the mountains of Zion;

For there the LORD commanded the blessing—

Life forevermore." (Psalm 133, NKJV)

There is divine order in everything God does. Notice the prerequisite for the oil being poured out: *dwelling together in unity*. This is true in marriages, families, and churches. The anointing will not be released on anything chaotic. Order attracts God's anointing. If there is strife in your marriage, then you do not qualify to receive a fresh anointing. Nothing works in your life, and prayer will become a struggle. You cannot argue your way out of a difficult situation. If you choose to be humble so as not to cause division, then the oil of the Holy Spirit will be poured on you and in your spirit.

You can have as much of God's power you can handle if you walk in God's order. It amazes me when people speak harshly about their parents or pastors. They do not know that by speaking against the order of God, they are disqualifying themselves from being anointed. The anointing will never work if you despise God's order. Each of us has a place that God designed for us in the home, the local church, and society. We must find out where our place is and exhibit a behaviour that complements our position. For instance, husbands are called to love their own wives. Well, if a husband speaks negatively about his wife, then he's not walking in love, is he? By speaking harshly about his wife, he steps out of the order God set in the home, and by doing so he steps outside of the anointing of God. Even His prayers will not be answered.

"Likewise, ye husbands, dwell with them according to knowledge, giving honour unto the wife, as unto the weaker vessel, and as being heirs together of the grace of life; **that your prayers be not hindered**." (1 Peter 3:7, KJV)

I am using this as an example so that you can see it's not just about prayer when it comes to tapping into the anointing of God within us. We must outwardly show a lifestyle that matches the anointing within us so that we cooperate with it and not oppose it, which is what we sometimes do.

Learn to work with the Holy Spirit so that the anointing flows out of you. ***Do not work against your anointing***.

Chapter Eleven: Confessions

The anointing in you responds to words of faith

"For with the heart one believes unto righteousness, and with the mouth **confession is made unto salvation**." (Romans 10:10, NKJV)

"And since we have the same spirit of faith, according to what is written, "I believed and therefore I spoke," **we also believe and therefore speak**." (2 Corinthians 4: 13-15, NKJV)

I hope by now you understand the importance of speaking God's word in *faith* to help release the anointing in you. Confess the following truths consistently until they become a reality in your everyday life.

Greater is He Who is in me than he who is in the world

I have received an anointing which abides in me

I am never without help

I can do all things through Christ Who strengths me

I pray without ceasing and make my connection with God through faith

I believe therefore I speak. I speak what is in my spirit. I base my confession on the Word of God and not circumstances

I walk by faith and not by sight

The power of God resides in me, and I tap into it through faith and prayer

I thank my God in everything and always praise Him

I will not quench the Holy Spirit Who lives in me

I look to the Holy Spirit for help and trust Him to lead me

I pray with my spirit, I also pray with my understanding

Christ is in me, the hope of glory. I have no guilt or shame abiding in me

The anointing of God in me teaches me all things

I am being strengthened each day

I refuse to be discouraged. I am of good courage because the greater One lives in me

I am more than a conqueror through Him Who loved me

Thanks be unto God Who always causes me to triumph

I walk with God every day, and His power is increasing in my life

The anointing in me destroys the work of the devil arrayed against me

The anointing of God in me reveals the mysteries of God as I continue to pray in the Spirit

The anointing of God will restore unto me everything the devil has stolen

Chapter Twelve: How to become Born-Again

You must be born again

"Do not marvel that I said to you, '**You must be born again**" (John 3:7, NKJV)

This is a profound statement made by Jesus Christ. The born-again experience, often referred 'the New Birth', is a Biblical experience that an individual has when he or she makes the decision to give their life to God having believed in the death, burial, and resurrection of Jesus Christ.

Many people may claim to be a Christian, and that's fine. One claims to be a member of this denomination, and another may have an allegiance to a different Christian affiliation; we all need to belong somewhere; however, the prerequisite for entry into the kingdom of God is being born again.

So, I ask you, have you been born again?

"Jesus answered and said to him, "Most assuredly, I say

to you, unless one is **born again**, he cannot see the

kingdom of God."

Before you can enjoy the benefits of the anointing within, you must have an assurance that you have been born again.

You cannot be born a Christian

Sure, you can be born into a professing Christian family who religiously observes a particular denomination's beliefs. You may even consider yourself to be a good person, you love your family, work hard, pay your taxes, etc. These are all good, but not good enough to give you access to eternal life. You see, not one of us is good enough.

"**There is none righteous**, no, not one;

There is none who understands;

There is none who seeks after God." (Romans 3:11,

NKJV)

Sin separated us from God, therefore God made His Son sin by sending Him to die for us. Jesus died our death. The punishment that we all deserved was put on Him. That way, God was able to separate us from our sin.

Jesus took our sin on the cross. What good news! Then God raised Jesus from the dead for our righteousness. Another way of saying righteousness is: 'right standing', or 'acceptance'.

You have a right standing with God when you become born again. All your sins are cleansed, and God gives you a new nature. The old has gone and the new has come.

This is more than a religious rite or a church ritual. When you give your life to Jesus and become born again, your spirit becomes alive to God.

"Therefore, if anyone is in Christ, he is a **new creation**; old things have passed away; behold, all things have become new." (2 Corinthians 5:17, NKJV)

It's so easy to be born again

So how do you become born again? Simple. Just do what the Bible says.

> "If you **confess with your mouth** the Lord Jesus and **believe in your heart** that God has raised Him from the dead, you will be saved." (Romans 10:9, NKJV)

All you need to do is believe in your heart! Then say it with your mouth. Tell God that you believe in His Son. Tell Him that you believe in what happened at the cross all those years ago, that Jesus died for your sin, and that He rose again from the dead and ascended to Heaven. Pray this prayer if you want to be born again:

'Father God, I come to you now in prayer and confess that Jesus Christ is Your Son and I believe with my heart that He died for me. I believe that You raised Your Son Jesus Christ from the dead. Cleanse me from every sin and iniquity in Jesus Name. I ask you to wash me clean from every wrong I have ever thought, said, and done; make me a new creation in Christ Jesus. I thank you for changing my nature and giving me Your Holy Spirit. Thank you that, according to Your Word, I am now born again.

If you've prayed the above prayer sincerely and in faith, then you really are born again. You've just begun a new chapter in your life and as you spend time reading the Bible and praying, God's will for you will become clearer. If you've made this decision and you'd like more information, you can call our office at GGMI, and we would love to be a blessing to you.

Chapter Thirteen: How to receive the Holy Spirit

If you have been born again, then you are ready to be filled with God's Spirit and speak with tongues. Let me tell you how I was filled with the Holy Spirit many years ago as I think it will help you receive this wonderful Gift.

My Testimony

I grew up in a nominal Christian and God-fearing home, like many in my neighbourhood, but had no personal understanding or revelation of who Jesus is and how to follow Him; nor was I interested. We were never religious although we observed the major Christian festivals and of course considered ourselves Christian. My turning point came in the summer of 1992 when I went inside a large church in London and gave my life to Jesus; that was quite a supernatural event. As I began to read my Bible following my new birth experience and attended church, I realised some were filled with the Holy Spirit and spoke in other tongues. I really wanted this experience since I saw it in the Bible and the early church practised it. I prayed and prayed for months with no result. I cried some evenings wondering why this experience was not granted to me and began to think maybe there was some grave sin in my life that was displeasing to the Lord and thought that's probably why I wasn't getting through to Him.

I asked people to pray for me; I had hands laid on me to receive. I even remember this minister who laid his scruffy hand on my immaculately groomed hair and messed it all up. I wouldn't have minded had I received, but I did not, or could not receive.

Long story short, a lady preacher visited our church and suggested to those of us who wanted to be filled with the Holy Spirit to come forward after the service and that she'd help us out. I did so, along some other seekers, and just stood there as her associate gave us some Bible verses. I was so disappointed since I'd expected for someone to at least pray for me, and God would zap me with a heavenly bolt of lightning. You see, my expectations were unscriptural. I was sincere, but I was sincerely unscriptural. And that's why I wasn't making my connection with God through prayer, and that's why many miss God's best because they focus on the spectacular.

You cannot connect with God apart from faith

The following morning, I knelt with my Bible and quoted to God the same verses that the preacher gave us the night before. I prayed a simple prayer, which I encourage you to pray also.

"And they were all filled with the Holy Spirit and **began to speak with other tongues**, as the Spirit gave them utterance." (Acts 2:4, NKJV)

I said, "Father, You said in Your Word that You give the Holy Spirit to everyone who asks. You said in Your Word that those who believe in Your Son, Jesus, will speak in tongues. You also said, '*and they were all filled with the Spirit and began to speak in other tongues.*' I now ask you to fill me with Your Spirit. I believe I have now received Your Spirit and I expect to speak in other tongues."

"And these signs will follow those who believe: In My name they will cast out demons; **they will speak with new tongues**..." (Mark 16:17, NKJV)

I did not finish the last couple of words before I spoke in other tongues. Many years have come and gone, and I'm still speaking in other tongues, enjoying this marvellous supernatural practise.

"If you then, being evil, know how to give good gifts to your children, how much more will your heavenly Father give the Holy Spirit to those who ask Him." (Luke 11:13, NKJV)

God wants you to be full of His Holy Spirit. You are a simple prayer away from receiving this wonderful Gift and the supernatural ability to speak in other tongues, which has a tremendous benefit in giving you spiritual strength and increasing the anointing of God in you.

"He who speaks in a tongue edifies himself." (1 Corinthians 14:4, NKJV)

About The Author

Michael Haile is an ordained minister and businessman with over twenty years' experience in the housing sector and ten years as an associate minister at Holiness unto the Lord International Church (UK), serving in the ministry of helps. He ministers through an international organisation he set up, Glorious Gospel Ministries International (GGMI), which sets the platform for him and others to preach the Gospel to the nations, equip churches, minister to the needy in prisons and orphanages, and anywhere else the Spirit of God leads. Michael's passion is to help men and women understand their rights and privileges in Christ and develop a personal relationship with their Saviour, with emphasis on the power of the Holy Spirit. He resides in London with his wife and children.

The Anointing Within, 2022

Author: Michael Haile (MBA), Pastor

GGMI, UK

www.g-gmi.org

Glorious Gospel Ministries International (GGMI)

GGMI was established in 2018 out of a wilderness experience and in response to the Lord's call "to open eyes that are blind,

to free captives from prison

and to release from the dungeon those who sit in darkness."

God is into the business of changing people's lives and the primary way He does that is through the teaching and preaching ministries. GGMI provides the platform for the gospel to go forth into the nations by organising city-wide evangelistic conferences, teaching seminars, business training for Christians; GGMI also works with partners to help develop communities including orphanages, water wells and prison ministries.

Printed in Great Britain
by Amazon